MW01201304

Investing in Tax Lien Houses in Missouri How to find Liens on Property

Buying Tax Lien Certificates Foreclosures in MO Real Estate Tax Liens Sales MO

by

Brian Mahoney

1

Join Our VIP Mailing List and Get FREE Money Making Training Videos! Then Start Making Money within 24 hours!
Plus if you join our Mailing list you can get Revised and New Edition versions of your book free!

And Notifications of other FREE Offers!

Just Hit/Type in the Link Below

https://mahoneyproducts.wixsite.com/win1

Get Our Video Training Program at:

**(Zero Cost Internet Marketing
complete 142 video series)
Amazing Training Videos!**

**YouTube Video Marketing
Email Marketing
Copy writing
Set up a Squeeze page
Getting Massive Web Traffic**

https://goo.gl/UFSIY6

Learn how to Get
Massive Money
for Real Estate Investing
@

http://www.BrianSMahoney.com

ABOUT THE AUTHOR

Brian Mahoney is the author of over 100 business start-up guides, real estate investing programs and Christian literature. He started his company MahoneyProducts in 1992.

He served in the US Army and worked over a decade for the US Postal Service. An active real estate investor, he has also served as a minister for the Churches of Christ in Virginia and Michigan.

He has degree's in Business Administration and Applied Science & Computer Programming.

His books and video training programs have helped thousands of people all over the world start there own successful business.

http://www.briansmahoney.com/

DEDICATION

**This book is dedicated to my Father
Ulester Love Mahoney Sr.
Thank you for all your sacrifice.**

ACKNOWLEDGMENTS

I WOULD LIKE TO ACKNOWLEDGE ALL THE HARD WORK OF THE MEN AND WOMEN OF THE UNITED STATES MILITARY, WHO RISK THEIR LIVES ON A DAILY BASIS, TO MAKE THE WORLD A SAFER PLACE.

Disclaimer

This book was written as a guide to starting a business. As with any other high yielding action, starting a business has a certain degree of risk. This book is not meant to take the place of accounting, legal, financial or other professional advice. If advice is needed in any of these fields, you are advised to seek the services of a professional.

While the author has attempted to make the information in this book as accurate as possible, no guarantee is given as to the accuracy or currency of any individual item. Laws and procedures related to business are constantly changing.

Therefore, in no event shall Brian Mahoney, the author of this book be liable for any special, indirect, or consequential damages or any damages whatsoever in connection with the use of the information herein provided.

Table of Contents

CHAPTER 1

TAX LIENS
&
TAX DEEDS

1. ALL ABOUT TAX LIEN CERTIFICATE SALES

A tax lien sale is the sale, conducted by a governmental agency, of tax liens for delinquent taxes on real estate. It is one of two methodologies used by governmental agencies to collect delinquent taxes owed on real estate, the other being the tax deed sale.

I. Sale process

In a tax lien sale, the lien (for delinquent taxes, accrued interest, and costs associated with the sale) is offered to prospective investors at public auction. Traditionally, auctions were held in person; however, Internet-based auctions (especially within large counties having numerous liens) have grown in popularity as this method allows for bidders from outside the area to participate.

In the event that more than one investor seeks the same lien, depending on state law the winner will be determined by one of five methods:

Bid Down the Interest. Under this method, the stated rate of return offered by the government is the maximum rate of return allowed. However, investors can accept lower rates of return, including zero percent in some cases (though this is rare in practice). The investor accepting the lowest rate of return is the winner. In the event more than one investor will accept the same lower rate, a random or rotational method (see below) will be used to break ties. (Florida and Arizona use this method)

Premium. Under this method, the investor willing to pay the highest "premium" (or excess above the lien amount) will be the winner. The premium may or may not earn interest, and may or may not be paid back to the investor upon redemption of the lien. (Colorado uses this method)

Random Selection. Under this method, a bidder will be randomly selected from those offering a bid. Usually a computer is used to make the selection, but in smaller jurisdictions more rudimentary methods may be used. Nevada uses Random selection since it is supposed to be the first buyer but it is hard to determine who was the first person to the sale.

Rotational Selection. Under this method, the first lien offered for sale will be offered to the investor holding bidder number one, who has the right of first refusal. If bidder number one refuses the lien, bidder number two may then bid. However, bidder number one will not be offered another lien until his number comes up again in the rotation. The next lien will go to the next number in line. Under this method, the investor has virtually no control over which liens s/he will obtain in the bidding, except to take or refuse what is offered.

Bid Down the Ownership. Used in Iowa and few other states, the investor willing to purchase the lien for the lowest percent of encumbrance on the property will be awarded the lien. For example, a bidder may agree to take a lien on only 95% of the property. If the lien is not redeemed, the investor would only receive 95% ownership of the property with the remaining 5% owned by the original owner. In practice, few investors will bid on liens for less than full right to the property or sale proceeds. Therefore, with multiple owners bidding on 100% encumbrance, the process then generally reverts to the random selection.

Liens not sold at auction are considered "struck" (or sold) to the entity (usually the county) conducting the auction. Some states allow "over the counter" purchases of liens not sold at auction.

II. Redemption process

The investor must wait a specified period of time (referred to as the "redemption period"), during which time the lien (plus interest and any other fees) may be repaid. Usually the lien holder is not permitted during this period to contact the property owner (or anyone else having an interest in the property, such as the mortgage holder) to demand payment or threaten foreclosure, or else the certificate can be forfeit.

In some jurisdictions, the lien holder must agree to pay subsequent unpaid property taxes during the redemption period in order to protect his/her interest. If the lien holder does not pay such taxes, a subsequent lien holder would "buy out" the prior lien holder's interest.

Once the redemption period is over, the lien holder may initiate foreclosure proceedings. The proceedings (the costs of which must be paid by the lien holder, though a redeeming property owner may be required to pay them as part of redemption) may result in either acquiring title to the property (normally this will be in the form of a quitclaim deed) or a tax deed sale of the property where the lien holder has the right of first bid (and may participate by making additional bids if s/he so chooses).

In Illinois a "Tax Deed" delivers a clean title as the court removes all clouds on title in the order directing the issuance of the deed. During the period between the initiation of proceedings and actual foreclosure, the property owner still has the opportunity to repay the lien with interest plus the costs incurred to foreclose.

If the lienholder does not act within a specified period of time, as defined by state law, the lien is forfeited and the holder loses his investment. This period of time ranges anywhere from 7 to 10 years and cannot be extended unless the taxlien is officially in the process of a tax deed application of Judicial Foreclosure.

A lien issued in error of state law is repaid, but usually at a far lower interest rate than had the lien been valid.

III. Benefits of tax lien investing

The maximum rate of return on a tax lien can be far higher than other investments. For example, Florida offers a maximum rate of 18% (1.5% per month, with a guaranteed 5% return regardless of time held), while Arizona offers a maximum rate of 16%. Iowa offers a guaranteed 2% per month (or 24% annual return).

IV. Pitfalls of tax lien investing

Payment is usually required at purchase or within a very short time afterward (often no more than 24–72 hours). Failure to pay the full amount results in all lien certificates purchased by the investor being cancelled, and may result in the investor losing his/her deposit and/or being barred from future sales.

In many states, further actions must be taken to protect the lien holder's rights after purchase of a lien, and generally within a certain period of time; failure to comply exactly with such requirements may make the lien worthless.

In "bid down the interest" jurisdictions, valuable properties are usually bid to the lowest rate possible greater than zero percent. (For example, Florida permits the interest rate to be bid down to a minuscule 0.25% – though it guarantees a minimum 5% return – while Arizona allows the bid to be as low as 1%.) Similarly, in "premium" states, valuable properties are bid up above the means of an average investor.

Unlike a certificate of deposit, tax liens are illiquid. They cannot be "cashed in" (resold to the taxing authority), but must be held until either they are repaid or the holder takes action to foreclose. (It is possible, however, to assign one's interest in a tax lien to another party.)

Tax Lien properties sold in non-Judicial Foreclosure states are conveyed to the highest bidder via a tax deed. The holder of the tax deed would then have to file a quiet title action, in the county where the property is situated, to clear of title defects. Although properties sold on tax deeds can be transferred, all financial institutions require a marketable title on property they will be financing.

Tax Liens that you hold on properties may become worthless due to municipal liens and assessments on the property. These liens and assessments (and their related interest) can increase the monies owed to a point that the property is deemed worthless.

2. ALL ABOUT TAX DEED SALES

A tax deed sale is the forced sale, conducted by a governmental agency, of real estate for nonpayment of taxes. It is one of two methodologies used by governmental agencies to collect delinquent taxes owed on real estate, the other being the tax lien sale.

Tax deed sale process

Real estate taxes are considered delinquent if not paid within a specified period of time. If the taxes are not paid, after legal requirements are met (such as giving proper notice to the property owner as well as others holding an interest in the property, or by filing required action in the courts), the property is offered for sale at a public auction.

At the sale, the minimum bid is generally the amount of back taxes owed plus interest, as well as costs associated with selling the property. In the event the property is not purchased, title may revert to the governmental entity that offered the property for sale. Title is generally transferred in a tax deed sale through a form of limited warranty or quitclaim deed (sometimes styled as Tax Deed or Sheriff's Deed); the purchaser would most likely then need to initiate a quiet title action in order to resell the property later (as a quitclaim deed is generally insufficient to acquire title insurance). However, the property can be sold from one investor to another by cash or owner financing using a limited warranty, Sheriff's Deed, or even a quitclaim deed.

Some jurisdictions allow for a post-sale "redemption period," whereby the former owner has a specified amount of time to reclaim the property by repaying the amount bid at auction plus a penalty. For example, Texas allows a 6-month (for non-homestead, non-agricultural properties) or two-year period (homestead or agricultural properties), with a flat 25% penalty to be added to the amount paid at the sale (50% after the first year), while Tennessee allows a full year, with a 10% penalty. As such, purchasers of properties at tax deed sales are cautioned not to make major improvements on the property until after the redemption period has expired.

A tax deed sale may also be used in conjunction with a tax lien, whereby the lienholder (instead of a governmental agency) starts the process toward forcing a public sale of the property. In those instances the lienholder's investment (the price of the lien plus any additional costs necessary to start the tax deed sale process, such as required fees and payment of any still-unpaid taxes or buyout of other certificate holders' interests) constitutes the minimum bid;

 if no other bids are received at the sale then the lienholder will take title to the property subject to redemption periods (if applicable) or any lawsuit to overturn the sale (for example, failure to provide proper notice).

Chapter 2

Finding Real Estate in Missouri

Quick & Easy Access to Foreclosure Real Estate

Getting Started

When Investing in Missouri first you have to determine what county you want to purchase in. To help you decide, below is a list of all counties in Missouri with their population and square miles. After the list of all the counties, you get a Goldmine Rolodex of web site address of Wholesale Government Tax Sale Properties and More!

Missouri Counties	Population	Square Miles
Saint Louis County	1,000,438	508
Jackson County	674,158	605
Saint Charles County	360,485	561
Saint Louis City	319,294	61.9
Greene County	275,174	675
Clay County	221,939	396
Jefferson County	218,733	657
Boone County	162,642	685
Jasper County	117,404	640
Franklin County	101,492	922

Missouri Counties	Population	Square Miles
Cass County	99,478	699
Platte County	89,322	420
Buchanan County	89,201	410
Christian County	77,422	563
Cole County	75,990	392
Cape Girardeau County	75,674	579
Saint Francois County	65,359	450
Newton County	58,114	626
Johnson County	52,595	831
Lincoln County	52,566	630
Pulaski County	52,274	547
Taney County	51,675	632
Phelps County	45,156	673
Callaway County	44,332	839
Camden County	44,002	655
Butler County	42,794	698
Pettis County	42,201	685

Missouri Counties	Population	Square Miles
.Howell County	40,400	928
Scott County	39,191	421
Lawrence County	38,634	613
Webster County	36,202	593
Barry County	35,597	779
Laclede County	35,571	766
Lafayette County	33,381	629
Warren County	32,513	432
Stone County	32,202	463
Dunklin County	31,953	546
Polk County	31,137	637
.Stoddard County	29,968	827
Marion County	28,781	438
Texas County	26,008	1,179
Adair County	25,607	568
Audrain County	25,529	693
Randolph County	25,414	482

Missouri Counties	Population	Square Miles
Washington County	25,195	760
Miller County	24,748	592
Crawford County	24,696	743
Ray County	23,494	570
Nodaway County	23,370	877
Saline County	23,370	756
McDonald County	23,083	540
Henry County	22,272	702
Vernon County	21,159	834
Clinton County	20,743	419
Morgan County	20,565	598
Benton County	19,056	706
Perry County	18,971	475
New Madrid County	18,956	678
Wright County	18,815	682
Pike County	18,516	673
Pemiscot County	18,296	493

Missouri Counties	Population	Square Miles
Ste. Genevieve County	18,145	502
Cooper County	17,601	565
Andrew County	17,291	435
Bates County	17,049	848
Dallas County	16,777	542
Dent County	15,657	754
Moniteau County	15,607	417
Macon County	15,566	804
Gasconade County	15,222	520
Livingston County	15,195	535
Mississippi County	14,358	413
Ripley County	14,100	630
Cedar County	13,982	476
Osage County	13,878	606
Douglas County	13,684	815
Wayne County	13,521	761
DeKalb County	12,892	424

Missouri Counties	Population	Square Miles
Linn County	12,761	620
Barton County	12,402	594
Bollinger County	12,363	621
Montgomery County	12,236	539
Madison County	12,226	497
Oregon County	10,881	792
Iron County	10,630	551
Grundy County	10,261	436
Lewis County	10,211	505
Ralls County	10,167	471
Howard County	10,144	466
Saint Clair County	9,805	677
Ozark County	9,723	747
Hickory County	9,627	399
Caldwell County	9,424	429
Carroll County	9,295	695
Maries County	9,176	528

Missouri Counties	Population	Square Miles
Harrison County	8,957	725
Monroe County	8,840	646
Shannon County	8,441	1,004
Daviess County	8,433	567
Dade County	7,883	490
Chariton County	7,831	756
Clark County	7,139	507
Gentry County	6,738	492
Sullivan County	6,714	651
Reynolds County	6,696	811
Shelby County	6,373	501
Carter County	6,265	508
Atchison County	5,685	545
Putnam County	4,979	518
Holt County	4,912	462
Scotland County	4,843	438
Schuyler County	4,431	308

Missouri Counties	Population	Square Miles
Knox County	4,131	506
Mercer County	3,785	454
Worth County	2,171	266

Missouri Wholesale Tax Sale Properties

As of the writting of this book, all of these websites are up and running. From time to time some will change their address. If a site does not come up sometimes using the root of the address works. For example if **www.mystate.gov/**greatdealcounty does not work. Just go with **www.mystate.gov**.

Boone County

https://www.showmeboone.com/collector/delinquent.asp

Camden County

https://goo.gl/z1leAM

Greene County

https://greenecountymo.gov/collector/tax_sale/index.php

Taney County

https://goo.gl/3tNBri

Missouri Tax Sale Property

Saint Louis County

St. Louis County Collector
41 South Central Ave., Clayton, MO 63105
Phone (314)615-5500

Jackson County

Jackson County Collector
415 East 12th St., First Floor, Kansas City, MO 64106
Phone (816)881-3232

https://www.16thcircuit.org/delinquent-land-tax

ST. Charles County

http://www.sccmo.org/283/Tax-Sale-Information

Clay County

https://www.claycountymo.gov/Collector/Tax_Sale

Missouri Real Estate Web Sites

http://www.mls.com/search/missouri.mvc

This web site has several links to real estate in Missouri counties and individual cities right on it's landing page!

http://www.realtor.com/realestateandhomes-search/Missouri

This web site has more links to real estate in Missouri counties and individual cities right on it's landing page!

Nationwide Real Estate Information

http://www.statelocalgov.net/50states-tax-authorities.cfm

http://www.brbpub.com/free-public-records/

www.RealAuction.com

www.GrantStreet.com

Locate Nationwide Tax Sale Properties

http://www.bid4assets.com/

Bid4assets is an amazing website for quickly finding investment property. The landing page has a map of the United States and you can just move your mouse pointer over the state you are interested in to see if they have any property in their database.

Here are just a few of assets you can target on this site!

* County Tax Sales

* Bank Owned Property

* US Marshal

* Real Estate

* Coins

* $1 No Reserve Homes

Locate Nationwide Tax Sale Properties

Http://www.realauction.com

Real Auction is another great website for instant access to property information.

Once on the landing page click "client sites".

They have 4 categories of information.

* Tax Liens Auctions

* Tax Deeds Applications

* Foreclosure and Tax Deed Auctions

* Tax Deed Management

Then chose from the states and counties that appear, that they have auction information.

Nationwide Banks & Foreclosure Properties

Bank of America

http://foreclosures.bankofamerica.com/

Wells Fargo

https://reo.wellsfargo.com/

Ocwen Financial Corporation

http://www.ocwen.com/reo

Hubzu

http://www.hubzu.com/

Government Foreclosure Properties

Fannie Mae
The Federal National Mortgage Association

https://www.fanniemae.com/singlefamily/reo-vendors

CHAPTER 3

FINANCING REAL ESTATE

8 Realistic Ways to Finance Real Estate

FINANCING REAL ESTATE

Welcome to Expert financing. I am going to show you several realistic ways to finance real estate. You are going to learn how to finance real estate with.

* VA LOANS

* PARTNERS

* INVESTMENT CLUBS

* CREDIT CARDS

* CORPORATE CREDIT

* EQUITY

* SELLER FINANCE

* HARD MONEY LENDERS

* AND FINALLY I SHOW YOU THE MONEY$!!

USING A VA LOAN

According to the web sites www.benefits.va.gov and www.military.com the current VA Loan amount is a whopping $417,000! What a lot of veterans don't know is that you can use that money to purchase not only your home, but investment properties. That is how I started my investing career. Purchasing multiple homes using my VA Loan.

FINANCING REAL ESTATE

Even if you are not a veteran, you can still partner up with one, who still has some money left on his or her VA LOAN.

If you are a Veteran, you will need to obtain a copy of your DD 214 and VA Form 26-1880 Request for a Certificate of Eligibility.

PARTNERS

This is another way I purchased a home. At the time I worked for the United States Postal Service. I had already purchased plenty of homes, so many of the workers were aware I had successfully invested in real estate. At break time I went around and ask people to partner up with me. I had multiple people offer to go in as a partner. I choose one and that house we rehabbed and flipped just two months after purchasing it. To this day it was the biggest gross profit on one deal, I have had. True I had to split it with my partner, but I would rather have half of something than all of nothing.

Having the combined resources of two people can be a great benefit, but it is not without it's challenges. If you are going to use a partner, no matter how close you are...GET EVERY THING IN WRITING.

FINANCING REAL ESTATE

Having a partner can dramatically increase the chance of a Bank lending money as well as having someone to split the work on rehabbing, should you decide to save money and make repairs yourself. But all this must be spelled out BEFORE you enter into a Agreement/Contract and purchase a home.

It helps if the person is like minded and understands the risks and benefits of investing, and truly understands the return on investment of a particular deal.

REAL ESTATE INVESTMENT CLUBS

Real estate investment clubs are groups that meet locally and allow investors and other professionals to network and learn. They can provide extremely useful information for both the novice and expert real estate investor. A top real estate club can provide a great forum to network, learn about reputable contractors, brokers, realtors, lawyers, accountants and other professionals. On the other hand, there are many real estate clubs designed to sell you. They bring in "gurus" who sell either on stage or at the back of the room, and as a result, the clubs typically profit to the tune of %50 of the sale price of the product, bootcamp, or training that is pitched.

FINANCING REAL ESTATE

I have purchased a ton of real estate books and real estate courses. Carlton Sheets, Dave Del Dotto, The Mylands, Seminar courses and much much more. I am not against any club bringing in a speaker who has a course. However I think there should be transparency to the members of the club.

There is certainly value in the networking that may come at one of these groups. But attend working to attain your goals and not necessarily the club's goal to sell you something. Some times both are the same thing. As a rule I usually leave debit cards at home the first time I attend an event. If there is a seller there with a "This day only offer" then I won't feel pressured to purchase. Plus most sellers can be convinced to sell at the discount offer price at a later time when you have had a chance to come down off the "sense of urgency emotional pitch" .

CREDIT CARDS

When using a credit card in real estate you must really do your homework on the deal. Dan Kennedy a world famous marketer once said "always stack the numbers in your favor". That's how you use a credit card. Look at the return on investment as compared to the long term cost of using a credit card and it's interest. Also I would recommend buying low cost homes that you can purchase and own free and clear.

FINANCING REAL ESTATE

No Mortgage Payment!!! My last 2 homes I have purchased have been cash deals. One home cost $1,500 and the other about $7,000. The first was a government property from HUD and the 2nd From a Bank. These institutions are unemotional about real estate and simply view a property as a non performing asset. The 2nd home was 4 bedrooms, 1 1/2 bath and a basement located in a farming community and came with a 2 car garage/shed and .6 acre(that is the size of a NFL football field) of land.

Later in this book I will show you how to find plenty of houses with amazing below wholesale prices and a formula for almost always finding a great deal.

CORPORATE CREDIT

Many people set up corporations to buy and sell real estate as an additional protection against liabilities. Other's create a corporation to mask personal involvement in property transfers and public records. Regardless of the use of a corporation, you can buy real estate with corporate credit as an alternative to using your own cash or IRA. By capitalizing on the credit rating of your corporation, you can buy real estate and build your corporate holdings portfolio.

FINANCING REAL ESTATE

Just remember that you can set up your corporation in a state that favors you the most for your real estate deals. Do your research. Most people like Delaware and Nevada, but you will have to decide if your home state or any other state is best for you and your business.

CURRENT EQUITY

Using the equity in your home for real estate investing is another way you can finance properties. You might use the money for a down payment or it may only be enough to cover the cost of some rehab repairs.

If you stick to the low cost home formula, you may have enough to purchase the entire house. A house is an investment that should appreciate in value as well as give a great ROI (Return On Investment). Whether you decide to flip the property or rent it out for positive cashflow.

If you have equity and it's not doing anything, then you may decide to make it a "performing asset" and use it as part of your real estate finance program.

FINANCING REAL ESTATE

SELLER FINANCING

Seller finance is where the seller of a free and clear property becomes your bank along with being the seller.

Advantages:

You get to purchase the property on terms that may be more beneficial for you. Seller gets monthly payments and the benefit of treating the sale as an installment sale thus allowing them to defer any capital gains taxes that may be due.

Disadvantages:

You may be locked into a mortgage with a pre-payment penalty or may not be able to resell the property immediately. This strategy is typically not meant for flipping but can definitely be used for that purpose if structured correctly.

Seller Finance is a known way to finance a property. That is why I have presented it in this book. But it is my least favorite because you now have a lingering relationship with your property. Your ability to make decisions regarding the property is limited and for that reason, I would don't go this route. However, like all types of financing, you have to ask yourself, "is the deal worth it."

FINANCING REAL ESTATE

I also prefer to work alone, but when a great deal came along, I sought out a partner to make it happen. Risk is usually relative to potential profit.

HARD MONEY LENDERS

A hard money lender is usually a individual or company that lends money for investment of a secured by the investment property.

Advantages:

Less red tape to get the money. You are dealing with people who understand the real estate investment business.

Disadvantage:

This is not a long term loan. The lender wants a return on investment, usually within a few months, a a year, or a few years. The interest rate on the loan is much higher than usual conventional banks.

Using hard money has a higher risk because the return on investment is due quicker. Therefore it is good idea not to use a Hard Money Lender, until you have a great deal of experience and confidence in being able to produce a return on investment.

SHOWING YOU THE MONEY

www.businessfinance.com (4,000 sources of money!)

www.advanceamericaproperty.com

http://www.cashadvanceloan.com/

www.brookviewfinancial.com

www.commercialfundingcorp.com

www.dhlc.com
(hard money for the Texas area)

www.equity-funding.com

www.bankofamerica.com

www.carolinahardmoney.com
(for real estate investors in North and South Carolina)

www.fpfloans.com

Chapter 4

Small Business Grants

How to write a Winning Grant Proposal

Small Business Grants

Government grants. Many people either don't believe government grants exist or they don't think they would ever be able to get government grant money.

First lets make one thing clear. Government grant money is **YOUR MONEY**. Government money comes from taxes paid by residents of this country. Depending on what state you live in, you are paying taxes on almost everything....Property tax for your house. Property tax on your car. Taxes on the things you purchase in the mall, or at the gas station. Taxes on your gasoline, the food you buy etc.

So get yourself in the frame of mind that you are not a charity case or too proud to ask for help, because billionaire companies like GM, Big Banks and most of Corporate America is not hesitating to get their share of **YOUR MONEY**!

There are over two thousand three hundred (2,300) Federal Government Assistance Programs. Some are loans but many are formula grants and project grants. To see all of the programs available go to:

http://www.CFDA.gov

WRITING A GRANT PROPOSAL

The Basic Components of a Proposal

There are eight basic components to creating a solid proposal package:

1. The proposal summary;

2. Introduction of organization;

3. The problem statement   (or needs assessment);

4. Project objectives;

5. Project methods or design;

6. Project evaluation;

7. Future funding; and

8. The project budget.

The Proposal Summary

The Proposal Summary is an outline of the project goals and objectives. Keep the Proposal Summary short and to the point. No more that 2 or 3 paragraphs. Put it at the beginning the proposal.

Introduction

The Introduction portion of your grant proposal presents you and your business as a credible applicant and organization.

Highlight the accomplishments of your organization from all sources: newspaper or online articles etc. Include a biography of key members and leaders. State the goals and philosophy of the company.

The Problem Statement

The problem statement makes clear the problem you are going to solve(maybe reduce homelessness). Make sure to use facts. State who and how those affected will benefits from solving the problem. State the exact manner in how you will solve the problem.

Project Objectives

The Project Objectives section of your grant proposal focus on the Goals and Desired outcome.

Make sure to identify all objectives and how you are going to reach these objectives. The more statistics you can find to support your objectives the better. Make sure to put in realistic objectives. You may be judged on how well you accomplish what you said you intended to do.

Program Methods and Design

The program methods and design section of your grant proposal is a detailed plan of action.

What resources are going to be used.

What staff in going to be needed.

System development

Create a Flow Chart of project features.

Explain what will be achieved.

Try to produce evidence of what will be achieved.

Make a diagram of program design.

Evaluation

There is product evaluation and process evaluation. The product evaluation deals with the result that relate to the project and how well the project has met it's objectives.

The process evaluation deals with how the project was conducted, how did it line up the original stated plan and the overall effectiveness of the different aspects of the plan.

Evaluations can start at anytime during the project or at the project's conclusion. It is advised to submit a evaluation design at the start of a project.

It looks better if you have collected convincing data before and during the program.

If evaluation design is not presented at the beginning that might encourage a critical review of the program design.

Future Funding

The Future Funding part of the grant proposal should have long term project planning past the grant period.

Budget

Utilities, rental equipment, staffing, salary, food, transportation, phone bills and insurance are just some of the things to include in the budget.

A well constructed budget accounts for every penny.

A complete guide for government grants is available at the website link below.

https://www.cfda.gov/downloads/CFDA.GOV_Public_User_Guide_v2.0.pdf

The guide can also be accessed at the very bottom of every page of the https://www.cfda.gov/ website.

Other sources of Government Funding

You can get General Small Business loans from the government. Go to the Small Business Administration for more information.

SBA Microloan Program

The Microloan program provides loans of up to $50,000 with the average loan being $13,000.

https://www.sba.gov/

CHAPTER 5

Buying Investment Property

Expert Strategies to Purchase Property

Expert Strategies to Purchase Property

AVOIDING & MANAGING & ELIMINATING RISK

Legendary Real Estate investor Dave Del Dotto once said "stick with the government, they will make you rich.". Real Estate is one of the safest investments in the world, when done properly. There is risk just driving to the grocery store. The only thing separating you from a head on collision is a yellow strip of paint. That being said, there are risks in every financial investment decision you make.

Do your research. Know what you want to do, before you begin. Are you looking to flip properties? Hold on and make money on the interest rates? Are you looking for a property to live in? Are you looking to rent out properties? Each decision requires a different type of research. If you are looking to rent out properties then you need to research what the local apartment complexes and homes are renting for in the area. If you are looking to flip a property then you need to find a real estate agent that can give you comps that have sole in the area within the past year.

Visit any property you are going to bid on. You do not want to get stuck with swampland or a unbuildable lot.

Expert Strategies to Purchase Property

AVOIDING & MANAGING & ELIMINATING RISK

You also don't want to get stuck with a property that has high property taxes. Learn the property tax rates of all the counties in the state that you are going to invest in.

Make sure that the property has not been condemned.

Make sure that the property does not have numerous costly violations of city codes.

Ask multiple real estate agents for information on any area you are interested in investing.

Ask about possible environmental issues.

Research possible liens by builders and contractors.

Beware of a owner who may declare bankruptcy on a property. This is a manageable risk but because laws change constantly, consult a real estate attorney for more information on how to handle this risk.

Avoid scams by dealing with government employees as much as possible.

Expert Strategies to Purchase Property

1. Decide how much you can afford to invest and stick with the numbers you come up with. Avoid something called Auction fever. It can be started by a "fast hammer". A fast hammer is when the auctioneer closes the auction early at a amazing price. It is designed to get your attention and get a fever about being the next one in the room to get a "Great Deal". When you go to a auction you should have a list of properties you have research and what your bid is going to be. This will help you to avoid Auction Fever.

2. Research. Single family homes with at least 3 bedrooms are great investments if purchased at the right price. Your research tells you what the right price is. Remember to use real estate agents and their access to the multiple listing service. Also many big companies like Remax and Century 21 have websites up with tons of information on the real estate area you wish to invest in.

www.trulia.com

 www.zillow.com

www.biggerpockets.com

https://www.census.gov/quickfacts/table/PST045216/00

http://www.realtor.org

Above are a few of the great sites to get research information on real estate.

Expert Strategies to Purchase Property

3. Get in contact with local counties for a list of delinquent properties for sale. Also ask when the sales will take place. Ask if you can be put on a mailing list. Use the internet to track down as much information as you can. Don't be afraid to use search engines other than Google. Bing and Yahoo are also great search engines to use.

4. Buy from other investors. Some people get in over their head. As long as you know the numbers and have research the property, it does not matter who you purchase it from as long as it is a good deal. One investor in Michigan recently purchased every single property for sale at a tax auction. He has to sell those properties or he is responsible for paying the taxes. As Carelton Sheets once said "you can't rationalize murder" so how can you rationalize why someone might offer you a great deal? Just do your due diligence on the property before making a deal.

5. Establish a relationship with local officials. Learn the names of the people who work in government offices that will be giving you information. Visit in person and say thank you. Call and say thank you. Send them a card that says thank you. How many people do you think do that for them? They will remember you. I worked for the government for over 20 years. I still remember the woman who repeatedly gave me lemon-aid when it was hot outside.

Expert Strategies to Purchase Property

6. Buy early in the Year. When you buy a tax lien certificate, back taxes have to be paid to the treasurer as well as interest and penalties. Redeem the property and you could be earning interest on this larger amount of money. If the property is not redeemed you can turn in the tax lien certificate and be handed a deed for the property, any extra amount you pay for the certificate comes from you because you could have gotten the same property for less.

7. Try smaller counties you may have much less competition.

8. Invest in your comfort zone. Try to find mentors who have already done what it is you want to do. As your knowledge and experience increases then you can take on bigger projects.

9 Write down your goals. Remember to answer the question of why you are doing this in the first place. A powerful why will keep you motivated when it comes time to do the legwork required to be successful.

10.   Take Action. There are plenty of smart people who are poor. Proper Knowledge plus action is the key to success.

Expert Strategies to Purchase Property

In microeconomics total cost (TC) describes the total economic cost of production and is made up of variable costs, which vary according to the quantity of a good produced and include inputs such as labor and raw materials, plus fixed costs.

In English... you factor in as many external costs, not just the cost of the investment property.

In order to be successful when buying investment property, you have to be good at determining the Total Cost of a property.

1. Get Investment Property Market Value

Wholesale Real Estate is real estate that is real estate priced under it's retail value. But how do you know that the retail value of real estate property? The standard formula for finding the value of real estate is to have a real estate agent find comparable (comps) properties that have sold recently. Usually about 4 properties with in a mile of the purchase property, that have sold within the past year. Formulas vary from bank to bank and real estate agent to real estate agent.

Today you can get a rough estimate by doing the research yourself. Remember that a bank will probably use their own formula, but at least you can try to get a ball park figure of a properties value by using the web sites below.

Expert Strategies to Purchase Property

Appraisal Web Sites

https://www.zillow.com/how-much-is-my-home-worth/

http://www.eppraisal.com/

2. Selecting a Real Estate Agent

So now that you have found a property, researched it's value, it's time to make an offer. As I mentioned in a earlier chapter of this book, some times you have to use a government approved agent to make an offer. Like any profession, there are good agents and not so good agents.

When I lived in Virginia, once a year the local paper published a list of all the top real estate agents for almost every real estate agent franchise/business. If your local paper does not do that then here is a formula I use for selecting a real estate agent.

Expert Strategies to Purchase Property

No part timers. Part time effort usually gets you part time results. I want an agent whose livelihood depends on their success.

Size Does Matter

The size that matters. The size or amount of properties sold. Not necessarily the gross amount of property value sold. Suppose you had a real estate agent who sold 1 million dollars worth of real estate and another who sold $500,000 worth of real estate. Which one do you choose? It depends. I want the agent who has sold the most individual properties, and not necessary the one who has the highest gross. An agent can sell only 1 house for a million dollars. The agent who sold $500,000 worth of real estate may have sold 10 $50,000 homes.

Usually a agent who makes a lot of sales has a good marketing formula in place and a good team of agents working with or for her/him. Don't be afraid to ask "who's your best agent? Why?". Often a real estate company will try to toss their worst agent a bone. Don't be that bone. Remember they work for you. Their commission comes the the property you are investing in.

Some courses teach you to negotiate the commission. I believe a proficient agent is worth the commission they desire. It's your job to select a good one.

Expert Strategies to Purchase Property

3. "100-3" Formula

Here is a quick and easy formula for getting a great deal on a real estate investment property, using a real estate agent that you have build up some rapport with.

Have the agent find 100 properties for sale that have been on the market for at least 90 days. Have the agent fax an offer of 25% below market value to all of the properties. Because the properties has been on the market for at least 90 days, you are dealing with a more motivated seller. It is likely that 10 out of the 100 will accept your offer. Now filter through the 10 and select the best 3 properties. Use these filters to help you select the best 3.

Strategies To Making Offers

1. What are the property taxes?

2. Are the any Homeowner Association dues?

3. What will be the appreciation value?

4. What will be your utility expenses.

5. How much will it cost, to be live in ready.

6. Is it the lowest valued house in the neighboorhood?

7. Crime Rate

Expert Strategies to Purchase Property

Property Taxes

I once owned two homes free and clear. The homes were in the same state. Both were similar in size, but one had a $3,000 a year property tax and the other one was $300 a year in property taxes. You can guess which one I moved first. Property taxes are often overlooked, but can be a big factor in the (TC) total cost. Due your research before you make an offer.

HOA

Usually when a house seems like the perfect deal, but has been sitting on the market for a long time, look to see what the HOA dues are. Personally I stay away from any property that has HOA dues, because they can escalate and you have no control over them.

Appreciation

Look at the history of real estate appreciationiation. It can vary greatly form city to city, and neighborhood to neighborhood. If you are going for a quick flip then this is not that important.

Utility Expenses

The importance of the expense depends on what you are going to do with the property.

Expert Strategies to Purchase Property

Rehab Expenses

If you are not an expert, have a professional inspect the house so you can factor in, a accurate estimate of rehab expenses. Be aware of any possible code violations as well.

Cost relative to the Neighborhood

Usually it's easiest to sell the cheapest house in the most expensive neighborhood. However if you just plan on renting the house then this is not as big a factor.

Crime Rate

The crime rate can have a big impact on resale value. Use web sites like https://www.crimereports.com/ to help understand it's impact on your property.

Expert Strategies to Purchase Property

4. "Take what the defense gives you"

Take what the defense gives you is a sports metaphor for viewing the landscape of a situation and adapting to what you see.

Take a similar approach to making offers in real estate. If you tell a "For Sale By Owner" everything that is wrong with the house he or she spend a lifetime building... you may insult the owner and lose the deal.

However, you send a list of needed repairs to a HUD representative, he may reduce the price of the property, no questions asked.

Adjust your offer making strategy to the person or organization you are dealing with. The farther removed a person is from the property, the less emotional they are about making deals.

Know your profit numbers and stick to them. Especially if you are bidding on a property. Be aware of Auction fever. It will bring out the competitive nature in you and can lead to you over bidding on a property. Know your numbers and be disciplined. The reason you pick out 3 properties in the 100-3 formula is so that you have 2 other properties to go to, if your first choice does not work out.

Chapter 6

HOW TO SELL YOUR HOUSE FAST!

12 Steps to Selling Any Property Fast!

HOW TO SELL YOUR HOUSE FAST!

12 Steps to Selling Any Property Fast!

1. Clean and Paint the house

Make sure the house is clean and uncluttered. This makes it easier for buyer to envision themselves living there. Make the bathrooms and kitchen a priority.

2. Scent the house

You might use a light incent or place some vanilla extract and place it on a old school lightbulb to give it a fresh baked cookie smell.

3. Write a property description

Writing a great property description is key to getting buyers interested in your home. One short cut to learning how to write a good property description is to view property listings of sold properties.

4. Take Good pictures

If you don't have a good camera, buy one. A picture is worth a 1,000 words.

HOW TO SELL YOUR HOUSE FAST!

12 Steps to Selling Any Property Fast!

5. Send a email to your buyers list

If you do not have a buyer's list, here is a link to a complete set of training videos on how to build a valuable customer list.

https://goo.gl/UFSIY6

6. Post ads on craigslist

Keep reposting your ads on a daily basis so that you stay at the top of the search results.

7. Post ads to http://www.backpage.com/

This is a Worldwide Classified Ad Web Site.

HOW TO SELL YOUR HOUSE FAST!

12 Steps to Selling Any Property Fast!

8. Place a Ad on http://realeflow.com/

This is the number one source for real estate investing leads.

9. https://www.zillow.com/rental-manager/

This is a free rental web site.

10. Create a video virtual tour

Create a video virtual tour and upload the video to YouTube. This is a powerful tool. YouTube is 2nd only to Google as the largest Search Engine in the world. However just posting a video won't get it seen. It has to be Search Engine Optimized(SEO). Below is a link to training videos that will show you step by step how to create great videos and get massive traffic viewing them!

https://goo.gl/UFSIY6

HOW TO SELL YOUR HOUSE FAST!

12 Steps to Selling Any Property Fast!

11. Post an ad on facebook target a city

You can place an ad on Facebook and target the city that your property is in.

12. Place a Standard For Sale sign in the yard

If possible have flyers available as well.

13. Place addition white signs in the yard

Give more information and get more attention by placing more personal signs in the yard.

14. List property in the MLS

If you are not a real estate agent get one to do it for you.

HOW TO SELL YOUR HOUSE FAST!

12 Steps to Selling Any Property Fast!

15. Place directional signs

Help people find your house. Make sure you are not violating any county codes when placing signs.

16. Continue marketing until closing

Don't slack off. If necessary you might want to hire VA's Virtual Assistants to keep all ads running.

17. Eliminating Negative Cash Flow

https://www.airbnb.com/

Airbnb is a web site that markets your house or rooms in your house for rent. It's easier to sell your house when it is clean, empty and buyers can envision themselves living in it.

However, if you are suffering from negative cash flow you might want to look into just renting out 1 room in the house.

HOW TO SELL YOUR HOUSE FAST!

12 Steps to Selling Any Property Fast!

18. ZERO COST MARKETING

Below are a few steps to market anything using ZERO COST INTERNET MARKETING STRATEGIES.

While there are many ways to market. In this section we are only going focus on ZERO COST MARKETING. When you are more established you can always go for the more expensive ways of marketing after your business is producing income.

FREE WEB HOSTING

Get a free web site. You can get a free web site at weebly.com or wix.com. Or just type "free web hosting" in a google, bing or yahoo search engine.

Free web hosting is something you can use for a variety or reasons. However many free web hosting sites add an extension to the name of your web address, and that lets everyone know you are using their services. For this reason you eventually want to scale up once you start making income.

LOW COST PAID WEB HOSTING

Free is nice, but you when you need to expand your business it is best to go with a paid web hosting service. There are several that give you good value for under $10.00 a month.

HOW TO SELL YOUR HOUSE FAST!

12 Steps to Selling Any Property Fast!

19. Low Cost Paid Web Hosting

1. Yahoo small business

2. Intuit.com

3. ipage.com

4. Hostgator.com

5. Godaddy.com

6. Webhosting pad

Yahoo small business allows for unlimited web pages and is probably the best overall value, but they require a years payment up front. Intuit allows for monthly payments.

For free ecommerce on your web site, open up a Paypal account and get the HTML code for payment buttons for free. Then put those buttons on your web site.

HOW TO SELL YOUR HOUSE FAST!

12 Steps to Selling Any Property Fast!

20. More Zero Cost Marketing

Step 1 zero cost internet marketing

Now that your web site is up and running you should register it with at least the top 3 search engines.

1. Google 2. Bing 3. Yahoo.

Step 2 zero cost internet marketing

Write and submit a press release. Google "free press release sites" for press release sites that will allow you to summit press releases for free. If you do not know how to write a press release go to www.fiverr.com and sub-contract the work out for only $5.00 !!!

Step 3 zero cost internet marketing

Write and submit articles to article marketing web sites like ezinearticles.com.

Step 4 zero cost internet marketing

Create and submit videos to video sharing sites like dailymotion.com or YouTube.com. Make sure to include a hyperlink to your website in the description of your videos.

Step 5 zero cost internet marketing

Submit your web site to dmoz.org. This is a huge open directory that many smaller search engines go to get web sites for their database.

Chapter 7

Millionaire Rolodex

Get Started Fast with these Business Web Sites

As of the writing of this book all, of the companies below, web site is up and have an active business. From time to time companies go out of business or change their web address. So, instead of just giving you just 1 source I give you plenty to choose from.

https://goo.gl/k6DU9k

hit the link above for an instant download of this book!:

YouTube Channel Passive Income Streams Video Marketing Book:

Build an Audience

with YouTube SEO & Make Money on YouTube

Top 15 Most Popular eBizMBA Rank

Real Estate Websites

Estimated Unique Monthly Visitors

1. **Zillow**   36,000,000

2. **Trulia**   23,000,000

3. **Yahoo! Homes**   20,000,000

4. **Realtor**   18,000,000

5. **Redfin**   6,000,000

6. **Homes**   5,000,000

7. **ApartmentGuide**   2,500,000

Top 15 Most Popular eBizMBA Rank

Real Estate Websites

Estimated Unique Monthly Visitors

8. **Curbed**   2,000,000

9. **ReMax**   1,800,000

10. **HotPads**   1,750,000

11. **ZipRealty**   1,600,000

12. **Apartments**   1,500,000

13. **Rent**   1,400,000

14. **Auction**   1,300,000

15. **ForRent**   1,200,000

Nationwide Banks & Foreclosure Properties

Bank of America

http://foreclosures.bankofamerica.com/

Wells Fargo

https://reo.wellsfargo.com/

Ocwen Financial Corporation

http://www.ocwen.com/reo

Hubzu

http://www.hubzu.com/

Government Foreclosure Properties

Fannie Mae
The Federal National Mortgage Association

https://www.fanniemae.com/singlefamily/reo-vendors

Department of Housing and Urban Development

https://www.hudhomestore.com/Home/Index.aspx

The Federal Deposit Insurance Corporation

https://www.fdic.gov/buying/owned/

The **United States Department of Agriculture**

https://properties.sc.egov.usda.gov/resales/index.jsp

United States Marshals

https://www.usmarshals.gov/assets/sales.htm#real_estate

Commercial Real Estate Properties

City Feet

http://www.cityfeet.com/#

The Commercial Real Estate Listing Service

https://www.cimls.com/

Land . Net

http://www.land.net/

Loop . Net

http://www.loopnet.com/

FSBO – For Sale By Owner

By Owner

http://www.byowner.com/

For sale by owner in Canada

http://www.fsbo-bc.com/

For sale by owner Central

http://www.fsbocentral.com/

For sale by Owner: world's largest FSBO web site

http://www.forsalebyowner.com/

Ranch by owner

http://www.ranchbyowner.com/

Tools to Get You Started Video Marketing

https://www.YouTube.com/

https://www.wikipedia.org/

https://screencast-o-matic.com/

http://www.openoffice.org/download/

Free Keyword Tools

https://adwords.google.com/home/tools/keyword-planner/

http://www.seocentro.com/

https://ubersuggest.io/

Promoting Your Real Estate/Videos

Top Free Press Release Websites

https://www.prlog.org

https://www.pr.com

https://www.pr-inside.com

https://www.newswire.com

https://www.OnlinePRNews.com

Social Media Websites

https://www.facebook.com

https://www.tumbler.com

https://www.pinterest.com

https://www.reddit.com

https://www.linkedin.com/

http://digg.com/

https://twitter.com

https://plus.google.com/

For Everything Under the Sun at Wholesale

http://www.liquidation.com/

COMPUTERS/Office Equipment

http://www.wtsmedia.com/

http://www.laptopplaza.com/

http://www.outletpc.com/

Computer Tool Kits

http://www.dhgate.com/wholesale/computer+repair+tools.html

http://www.aliexpress.com/wholesale/wholesale-repair-computer-tool.html

http://wholesalecomputercables.com/Computer-Repair-Tool-Kit/M/B00006OXGZ.htm

http://www.tigerdirect.com/applications/category/category_tlc.asp?CatId=47&name=Computer%20Tools

Computer Parts

http://www.laptopuniverse.com/

http://www.sabcal.com/

other

http://www.nearbyexpress.com/

http://www.commercialbargains.co

http://www.getpaid2workfromhome.com

http://www.boyerblog.com/success-tools

Small Business Resources

1. http://www.sba.gov/content/starting-green-business

2. http://www.sba.gov/content/home-based-business

3. online businesses

http://www.sba.gov/content/setting-online-business

4. self employed and independent contractors

http://www.sba.gov/content/self-employed-independent-contractors

5. minority owned businesses

http://www.sba.gov/content/minority-owned-businesses

6. veteran owned businesses

http://www.sba.gov/content/veteran-service-disabled-veteran-owned

7. woman owned businesses

http://www.sba.gov/content/women-owned-businesses

8. people with disabilities

http://www.sba.gov/content/people-with-disabilities

9. young entrepreneurs

http://www.sba.gov/content/young-entrepreneurs

CHAPTER 8

BILLIONAIRE BUSINESS ADVICE

When They Talk, We Listen.

There is a link to YouTube videos created

by Evan Carmichael

Billionaire Business Advice

Bill Gates...

1. Have Energy

2. Have a Bad Influence

3. Work Hard

4. Create the Future

5. Enjoy what you do

6. Play Bridge

7. Ask for Advice

8. Pick Good People

9. Don't Procrastinate

10.   Have a sense of Humor

https://goo.gl/KE5CBT

Billionaire Business Advice

Mark Zuckerberg...

1. You get what you spend your time doing

2. Get Feedback

3. Make Mistakes

4. Only hire people who you would work for

5. Make a change in the world

6. Learn from the people around you

7. Build a really good team

8. Give the very best experience

9. Care the most about it

10.   Social bonds are critical

   https://www.YouTube.com/watch?v=HMpWXQpogqI&t=125s

Billionaire Business Advice

Oprah Winfrey...

1. Understand the next right move

2. Seize your Opportunity

3. Everyone makes mistakes

4. Work on yourself

5. Run the race as hard as you can

6. Believe

7. We are all seeking the same thing

8. Find your purpose

9. Stay grounded

10.   Relax its going to be okay

https://www.YouTube.com/watch?v=7a8ncSBU-Eg

Billionaire Business Advice

Michael Jordan...

1. Keep Working Hard

2. Ignite the Fire

3. Be Different

4. Fail Your Way to Success

5. Have High Expectations

6. Be Positive

7. Be who you were born to be

8. Have a vision

9. Stop Making EXCUSES

10.   Practice

https://www.YouTube.com/watch?v=NidqtkXq9Yg&t=8s

Billionaire Business Advice

Holy Bible...

1. Have a vision:

"And the LORD answered me, and said, Write the vision, and make it plain upon tables, that he may run that readeth it" **Habakkuk 2:2**

2. Speak Life:

Death and life are in the power of the tongue: and they that love it shall eat the fruit thereof. **Proverbs 18:21**

3. Ask for what you want

Ye lust, and have not: ye kill, and desire to have, and cannot obtain: ye fight and war, yet ye have not, because ye ask not. **James 4:2**

4. Be willing to work for it

And he shall be like a tree planted by the rivers of water, that bringeth forth his fruit in his season; his leaf also shall not wither; and whatsoever he **doeth** shall prosper. **Psalm 1:3**

5. Accept Challenges

No discipline is fun while it lasts, but it seems painful at the time. Later, however, it yields the peaceful fruit of righteousness for those who have been trained by it. **Hebrews 12:11**

6. Give Back

Everyone should give whatever they have decided in their heart. They shouldn't give with hesitation or because of pressure. God loves a cheerful giver.

2 Corinthians 9:7

7. Tell the truth

But for the cowardly, the faithless, the vile, the murderers, those who commit sexual immorality, those who use drugs and cast spells, the idolaters and **all liars**—their share will be in the lake that burns with fire and sulfur. This is the second death."

Revelation 21:8

8. Reinvest your profits

In that case, you should have turned my money over to the bankers so that when I returned, you could give me what belonged to me with interest.

Matthew 25:27

9. Be thankful

"Give thanks to the Lord because he is good, because his faithful love lasts forever!"

Psalm 107:1

10.   Help others

The Samaritan went to him and bandaged his wounds, tending them with oil and wine. Then he placed the wounded man on his own donkey, took him to an inn, and took care of him.

Luke 10:34

Gold Medal Prayers: Brian Mahoney

https://goo.gl/GzeMAO

CHAPTER 9

REAL
ESTATE
TERMS

Acceleration Clause - A contract provision that allows a lender to require a borrower to repay all or part of an outstanding loan if certain requirements are not met. An acceleration clause outlines the reasons that the lender can demand loan repayment. Also known as "acceleration covenant".

Accrued Depriciation - Depreciation is the loss in value to any structure due to a variety of factors, such as wear and tear, age, and poor location. The term accrued depreciation means the total depreciation of a building from all causes.

Accrued Interest - In finance, accrued interest is the interest on a bond or loan that has accumulated since the principal investment, or since the previous coupon payment if there has been one already. For a financial instrument such as a bond, interest is calculated and paid in set intervals (for instance annually or semi-annually).

Active Income - Active income is income for which services have been performed. This includes wages, tips, salaries, commissions and income from businesses in which there is material participation.

Add-on Interest - A method of calculating interest whereby the interest payable is determined at the beginning of a loan and added onto the principal. The sum of the interest and principal is the amount repayable upon maturity.

Adjustable Rate Mortgage (ARM) - A variable-rate mortgage, adjustable-rate mortgage (ARM), or tracker mortgage is a mortgage loan with the interest rate on the note periodically adjusted based on an index which reflects the cost to the lender of borrowing on the credit markets.

Cash flow after taxes (CFAT) - Cash flow after taxes (CFAT) is a measure of financial performance that looks at the company's ability to generate cash flow through its operations. It is calculated by adding back non-cash accounts such as amortization, depreciation, restructuring costs and impairments to net income.

Agent - One who is legally authorized to act on behalf of another person.

Agreement for sale - An agreement of sale constitutes the terms and conditions of sale of a property by the seller to the buyer. ... Sale deed is the document prepared at the time of full payment made by the buyer and when the actual transfer of the property takes place.

Alienation clause - A clause in a mortgage contract that requires full payment of the balance of a mortgage at the lender's discretion if the property is sold or the title to the property changes to another person. Nearly all mortgages have an alienation clause.

All-inclusive deed of trust (AITD) - An All Inclusive Trust Deed (AITD) is a new deed of trust that includes the balance due on the existing note plus new funds advanced; also known as a wrap-around mortgage.

American Land Title Association (ALTA) -The American Land Title Association (ALTA) is a trade association representing the title insurance industry. Founded in 1907, ALTA also focus on a property's abstract of title, which ties the history of the title to a particular piece of real estate.

Amortization - Amortization is an accounting term that refers to the process of allocating the cost of an intangible asset over a period of time. It also refers to the repayment of loan principal over time.

Amortized loan - An amortized loan is a loan with scheduled periodic payments that consist of both principal and interest. An amortized loan payment pays the relevant interest expense for the period before any principal is paid and reduced.

Appraisal - an expert estimate of the value of something.

Appraised value - An appraised value is an evaluation of a property's value based on a given point in time that is performed by a professional appraiser during the mortgage origination process. The appraiser is usually chosen by the lender, but the appraisal is paid for by the borrower.

Appraiser - A practitioner who has the knowledge and expertise necessary to estimate the value of an asset, or the likelihood of an event occurring, and the cost of such an occurrence.

Arbitration - the use of an arbitrator to settle a dispute.

Arbitration clause - An arbitration clause is a clause in a contract that requires the parties to resolve their disputes through an arbitration process

Asking price - the price at which something is offered for sale.

Assessment - the evaluation or estimation of the nature, quality, or ability of someone or something.

Assignee - a person to whom a right or liability is legally transferred.

Assignment - An assignment (Latin cessio) is a term used with similar meanings in the law of contracts and in the law of real estate. In both instances, it encompasses the transfer of rights held by one party—the assignor—to another party—the assignee.

Assumption Clause - A provision in a mortgage contract that allows the seller of a home to pass responsibility to the buyer of the home for the existing mortgage. In other words, the new homeowner assumes the existing mortgage. There are typically many conditions and a fee required in an assumption clause.

Assumption of mortgage - Mortgage assumption is the conveyance of the terms and balance of an existing mortgage to the purchaser of a financed property, commonly requiring that the assuming party is qualified under lender or guarantor guidelines.

At-risk rule - Tax laws limiting the amount of losses an investor (usually a limited partner) can claim. Only the amount actually at risk can be deducted.

Authorization to sell - Authorization to sell is a listing contract whereby a representative is employed by a seller to secure a buyer for the property. An authorization to sell does not give the agent the authority to enter into a binding contract of sale.

Backup offer - A backup offer is when a home seller has accepted an offer from a buyer, but is still accepting offers from other buyers. Sellers state that they are accepting backup offers if they think the current offer may fall through

Balloon mortgage - a mortgage in which a large portion of the borrowed principal is repaid in a single payment at the end of the loan period.

Balloon payment - a repayment of the outstanding principal sum made at the end of a loan period, interest only having been paid hitherto.

Binder insurance - binder. A legal agreement issued by either an agent or an insurer to provide temporary evidence of insurance until a policy can be issued. Binders should contain definite time limits, should be in writing, and should clearly designate the insurer with which the risk is bound

Captial gain - a profit from the sale of property or of an investment.

Capitalization - the provision of capital for a company, or the conversion of income or assets into capita

Cash basis taxpayer - A taxpayer who reports income and deductions in the year that they are actually paid or received. Cash basis taxpayers cannot report receivables as income, nor deduct promissory notes as payments.

Cash flow - the total amount of money being transferred into and out of a business, especially as affecting liquidity.

Certificate of title - A certificate of title is a state or municipal-issued document that identifies the owner or owners of personal or real property. A certificate of title provides documentary evidence of the right of ownership.

Chattel - an item of property other than real estate.

Closing costs - Closing costs are fees paid at the closing of a real estate transaction. This point in time called the closing is when the title to the property is conveyed (transferred) to the buyer. Closing costs are incurred by either the buyer or the seller.

Cloud on title - Any document, claim, unreleased lien or encumbrance that might invalidate or impair the title to real property or make the title doubtful. Clouds on title are usually discovered during a title search. Clouds on title are resolved through initiating a quitclaim deed or a commencement of action to quiet title.

Co-insurance - a type of insurance in which the insured pays a share of the payment made against a claim.

Collateral - something pledged as security for repayment of a loan, to be forfeited in the event of a default.

Commission - A fee charged by a broker or agent for his/her service in facilitating a transaction, such as the buying or selling of securities or real estate. In the case of securities trading, brokers can be split into two broad categories depending on the commissions they charge.

Contract of sale - A real estate contract is a contract between parties for the purchase and sale, exchange, or other conveyance of real estate.

Cost approach - Cost approach. ... The fundamental premise of the cost approach is that a potential user of real estate won't, or shouldn't, pay more for a property than it would cost to build an equivalent. The cost of construction minus depreciation, plus land, therefore is a limit, or at least a metric, of market value.

Debt coverage ratio - In corporate finance, DSCR refers to the amount of cash flow available to meet annual interest and principal payments on debt, including sinking fund payments. In personal finance, DSCR refers to a ratio used by bank loan officers in determining debt servicing ability.

Declining balance method - A declining balance method is a common depreciation-calculation system that involves applying the depreciation rate against the non-depreciated balance.

Deed - A deed (anciently "an evidence") is any legal instrument in writing which passes, affirms or confirms an interest, right, or property and that is signed, attested, delivered, and in some jurisdictions, sealed. It is commonly associated with transferring (conveyancing) title to property.

Deed of trust - In real estate in the United States, a deed of trust or trust deed is a deed wherein legal title in real property is transferred to a trustee, which holds it as security for a loan (debt) between a borrower and lender. The equitable title remains with the borrower.

Depreciation - Depreciation is an accounting method of allocating the cost of a tangible asset over its useful life. Businesses depreciate long-term assets for both tax and accounting purposes.

Double escrow - Double escrow. ... Double escrow is a set of real estate transactions involving two contracts of sale for the same property, to two different back-to-back buyers, at the same or two different prices, arranged to close on the same day.

Due diligence - Due diligence means taking caution, performing calculations, reviewing documents, procuring insurance, walking the property, etc. — essentially doing your homework for the property BEFORE you actually make the purchase

Earnest money - Earnest money is a deposit made to a seller showing the buyer's good faith in a transaction. Often used in real estate transactions, earnest money allows the buyer additional time when seeking financing. Earnest money is typically held jointly by the seller and buyer in a trust or escrow account.

Eminent domain - Eminent Domain. The power of the government to take private property and convert it into public use. The Fifth Amendment provides that the government may only exercise this power if they provide just compensation to the property owners.

Encroachment - A situation in real estate where a property owner violates the property rights of his neighbor by building something on the neighbor's land or by allowing something to hang over onto the neighbor's property.

Equity participation - Equity participation is the ownership of shares in a company or property. ... The greater the equity participation rate, the higher the percentage of shares owned by stakeholders. Allowing stakeholders to own shares ties the stakeholders' success with that of the company or real estate investment.

Escrow - Escrow generally refers to money held by a third-party on behalf of transacting parties. ... It is best known in the United States in the context of real estate (specifically in mortgages where the mortgage company establishes an escrow account to pay property tax and insurance during the term of the mortgage).

Escrow instructions - n. the written instructions by buyer and seller of real estate given to a title company, escrow company or individual escrow in "closing" a real estate transaction. These instructions are generally prepared by the escrow holder and then approved by the parties and their agents. (See: closing, escrow)

Estoppel - Estoppel Certificate. An estoppel certificate is a document used in mortgage negotiations to establish facts and financial obligations, such as outstanding amounts due that can affect the settlement of a loan. It is required by a lender of a third party in a real estate transaction

Exclusive right to sell listing - An Exclusive Right to Sell/Lease means that the listing brokerage has an exclusive listing agreement with the Seller. (Sorry about using a word in the term to define the term!) It means that a commission would be owed to the Listing Brokerage when the property is sold to a buyer, regardless of who brings the buyer.

Fair market value - The fair market value is the price at which the property would change hands between a willing buyer and a willing seller, neither being under any compulsion to buy or to sell and both having reasonable knowledge of relevant facts.

Fee simple - In English law, a fee simple or fee simple absolute is an estate in land, a form of freehold ownership. It is a way that real estate may be owned in common law countries, and is the highest possible ownership interest that can be held in real property.

First right of refusal - A right of first refusal is a contractual right granted by an owner of property. The owner gives the holder of the right an opportunity to enter into a business transaction with the owner according to specified terms, before the owner may enter into that transaction with a third party.

Foreclosure - Foreclosure is a legal process in which a lender attempts to recover the balance of a loan from a borrower, who has stopped making payments to the lender, by forcing the sale of the asset used as the collateral for the loan.

Gift deed - Quitclaim Deed Vs. Gift Deed. Property deeds define and protect ownership in a home. In real estate, deeds are legal documents that transfer ownership of a property from one party to another. ... Each type of deed is used for a specific situation.

Grantee - In real estate, the grantee is the recipient of a property - the person who will be taking title, as named in the the legal document used to transfer the real estate. The person who is relinquishing the property is called the grantor.

Grantor - First, it's important to review the legal definition of "grantor" and "grantee." In a real estate transaction, the grantor is the party that conveys the property in question. The grantor may be an individual, business entity or partnership. The grantee is the party that receives the property

Gross income - A real estate investment term, Gross Operating Income refers to the result of subtracting the credit and vacancy losses from a property's gross potential income. Also Known As: Effective Gross Income (EGI)

Gross rent multiplier - Gross Rent Multiplier is the ratio of the price of a real estate investment to its annual rental income before accounting for expenses such as property taxes, insurance, utilities, etc.

Highest and best use - The Appraisal Institute defines highest and best use as follows: The reasonably probable and legal use of vacant land or an improved property that is physically possible, appropriately supported, financially feasible, and that results in the highest value.

House Flipping is a type of real estate investment strategy in which an investor purchases properties with the goal of reselling them for a profit. Profit is generated either through the price appreciation that occurs as a result of a hot housing market and/or from renovations and capital improvements.

Income approach to value - The income approach is a real estate appraisal method that allows investors to estimate the value of a property by taking the net operating income of the rent collected and dividing it by the capitalization rate.

Installment sale - A method of sale that allows for partial deferral of any capital gain to future taxation years. Installment sales require the buyer to make regular payments, or installments, on an annual basis, plus interest if installment payments are to be made in subsequent taxation years.

Insurable title - Marketable Title vs. Insurable Title. ... When a title is marketable it means that the chain of ownership (title) to a particular piece of property is clear and free from defects. And as such, it can be marketed for sale without additional effort by the seller or potential buyer.

Interest - Estates and ownership interests defined. The law recognizes different sorts of interests, called estates, in real property. The type of estate is generally determined by the language of the deed, lease, bill of sale, will, land grant, etc., through which the estate was acquired.

Internal rate of return (IRR) - is used in capital budgeting measuring the profitability of potential investments. Internal rate of return is a discount rate that makes the net present value (NPV) of all cash flows from a particular project equal to zero. ... r = discount rate, and. t = number of time periods

Involuntary lien - involuntary lien. A lien on real estate that results without the property owners' voluntary cooperation in the placement of the lien. Examples include tax liens and judgment liens. Contrast with a mortgage,which is voluntary.

Joint and several note - Joint and several note is a promissory note which is the note of all and of each of the makers as to its legal obligation between the parties to it.

Joint tenancy - A type of property right where two or more people own or rent a property together, each with equal rights and obligations, until one owner dies. Upon an owner's death, that owner's interest in the property passes to the survivors without the property having to go through probate.

Judgment proof - People are judgment-proof if they lack the resources or insurance to pay a court judgment against them. For example, suppose that a thief steals your car, sells it, and then burns all of his worldly possessions. Even if you sued him and won, you could not recover anything because the thief is judgment-proof.

Lease option - A lease option (more formally Lease With the Option to Purchase) is a type of contract used in both residential and commercial real estate. In a lease-option, a property owner and tenant agree that, at the end of a specified rental period for a given property, the renter has the option of purchasing the property.

Letter of credit - 1. INTRODUCTION. Letters of credit are often used in real estate transactions to secure obligations. ... For example, a tenant may request its bank to issue a letter of credit to the landlord as security. In such a transaction, the tenant is the applicant, the bank is the issuer and the landlord is the beneficiary.

Leverage - Leverage is the use of various financial instruments or borrowed capital to increase the potential return of an investment – and it is an extremely common term on both Wall Street and in the Main Street real estate market. (Learn more about the various uses of leverage in Leveraged Investment Showdown.)

Like kind property - Like-Kind Property. Any two assets or properties that are considered to be the same type, making an exchange between them tax free. To qualify as like kind, two assets must be of the same type (e.g. two pieces of residential real estate), but do not have to be of the same quality.

Limited partnership - RELP' A limited partnership entity organized to invest in real estate. A Real Estate Limited Partnership is typically organized with an experienced property manager or real estate development firm serving as the general partner.

Lis pendens - In United States law, a lis pendens is a written notice that a lawsuit has been filed concerning real estate, involving either the title to the property or a claimed ownership interest in it.

Loan to value - The loan to value or LTV ratio of a property is the percentage of the property's value that is mortgaged. ... Loan to Value is used in commercial real estate as well. Examples: $300,000 appraised value of a home. $240,000 mortgage on the property. $240,000 / $300,000 = .80 or 80% Loan to Value Ratio

Market value - Market value is the most probable price that a property should bring in a competitive and open market under all conditions requisite to a fair sale, the buyer and seller, each acting prudently, knowledgeably and assuming the price is not affected by undue stimulus.

Mechanics lien - A guarantee of payment to builders, contractors and construction firms that build or repair structures. Mechanic's liens also extend to suppliers of materials and subcontractors and cover building repairs as well.

Mortgage broker - A mortgage broker is an intermediary working with a borrower and a lender while qualifying the borrower for a mortgage. The broker gathers income, asset and employment documentation, a credit report and other information for assessing the borrower's ability to secure financing.

Multiple listing - A multiple listing service (MLS, also multiple listing system or multiple listings service) is a suite of services that real estate brokers use to establish contractual offers of compensation (among brokers) and accumulate and disseminate information to enable appraisals.

Net income - Net operating income (NOI) is a calculation used to analyze real estate investments that generate income. Net operating income equals all revenue from the property minus all reasonably necessary operating expenses

Net rentable area - Actual square-unit of a building that may be leased or rented to tenants, the area upon which the lease or rental payments are computed. It usually excludes common areas, elevator shafts, stairways, and space devoted to cooling, heating, or other equipment. Also called net leasable area.

Non-recourse note - Nonrecourse debt or a nonrecourse loan is a secured loan (debt) that is secured by a pledge of collateral, typically real property, but for which the borrower is not personally liable.

Obsolescence - Functional obsolescence is a reduction in the usefulness or desirability of an object because of an outdated design feature, usually one that cannot be easily changed. The term is commonly used in real estate, but has a wide application.

Option - A real estate purchase option is a contract on a specific piece of real estate that allows the buyer the exclusive right to purchase the property. Once a buyer has an option to buy a property, the seller cannot sell the property to anyone else.

Passive activity income - Internal Revenue Service (IRS) defines two types of passive activity: trade or business activities not materially participated in, and rental activities even if the taxpayer materially participated in them (unless the taxpayer is a real estate professional).

Point - In real estate mortgages, a point refers to the origination fee charged by the lender, with each point being equal to 1% of the amount of the loan. It can also refer to each percentage difference between a mortgage's interest rate and the prime interest rate.

Possession - A principle of real estate law that allows a person who possesses someone else's land for an extended period of time to claim legal title to that land.

Potential gross income - The amount of income produced by a piece of property, plus miscellaneous income, less vacancy costs and collection losses. Effective gross income is a metric commonly used to evaluate the value of a piece of investment property. ... The EGI for the property is $500,000 - $100,000, or $400,000.

Preliminary title report - A preliminary title sets forth various details about a piece of real estate, including: Ownership;

Liens and encumbrances; and Easements.

The information in a preliminary title report, also known as a title search, is gathered from the property records in the county where the property is located.

Prepayment penalty - Prepayment Penalty. A prepayment penalty is a clause in a mortgage contract stating that a penalty will be assessed if the mortgage is prepaid within a certain time period. The penalty is based on a percentage of the remaining mortgage balance or a certain number of months' worth of interest.

Principal - In commercial law, a principal is a person, legal or natural, who authorizes an agent to act to create one or more legal relationships with a third party.

Pro forma - What does 'Pro Forma' mean. Pro forma, a Latin term, literally means "for the sake of form" or "as a matter of form." In the world of investing, pro forma refers to a method by which financial results are calculated. This method of calculation places emphasis on present or projected figures.

Promissory note - In the United States, a mortgage note (also known as a real estate lien note, borrower's note) is a promissory note secured by a specified mortgage loan; it is a written promise to repay a specified sum of money plus interest at a specified rate and length of time to fulfill the promise.

Property management - Property management is the operation, control, and oversight of real estate as used in its most broad terms. Management indicates a need to be cared for, monitored and accountability given for its useful life and condition.

Quit claim deed - A quitclaim deed is a legal instrument which is used to transfer interest in real property. The entity transferring its interest is called the grantor, and when the quitclaim deed is properly completed and executed, it transfers any interest the grantor has in the property to a recipient, called the grantee.

Real estate owned (REO) - Real estate owned or REO is a term used in the United States to describe a class of property owned by a lender—typically a bank, government agency, or government loan insurer—after an unsuccessful sale at a foreclosure auction.

Real property - Real estate is "property consisting of land and the buildings on it, along with its natural resources such as crops, minerals or water; immovable property of this nature; an interest vested in this (also) an item of real property, (more generally) buildings or housing in general.

Realized gain - The amount by which the sale price of an asset exceeds its purchase price. Unless the realized gain came from a tax-exempt or tax-deferred asset, it is taxable. However, the type of taxation to which it is subject varies according to how long the asset has been owned. A realized gain from an asset owned longer than one year is usually taxed at the capital gains rate, while an asset owned for a period shorter than a year is often subject to the higher income tax rate. It is also called the recognized gain.

Refinancing - Getting a new mortgage to replace the original is called refinancing. Refinancing is done to allow a borrower to obtain a better interest term and rate. The first loan is paid off, allowing the second loan to be created, instead of simply making a new mortgage and throwing out the original mortgage.

Rental concession - Rental Concessions are benefits that are offered by the landlord to his tenants. Concessions are usually offered to draw tenants to vacant properties. Some other landlords may choose to offer a concession if the tenant decides to renew the lease. Even when the landlord is planning to sell a home, in return for his tenants co-operation he may offer incentives or concessions.

Replacement cost - A replacement cost is the cost to replace an asset of a company at the same or equal value, and the asset to be replaced could be a building, investment securities, accounts receivable or liens.

Reproduction cost - The costs involved with identically reproducing an asset or property with the same materials and specifications as an insured property based on current prices.

Rescission - Rescission is the cancellation of a real estate contract between the buyer and seller. The act of rescinding a contract will "unwind" the transaction specified in the contract. A real estate contract may be rescinded at varying points during a transaction.

Restrictive covenant - A restrictive covenant is any type of agreement that requires the buyer to either take or abstain from a specific action. In real estate transactions, restrictive covenants are binding legal obligations written into the deed of a property by the seller.

Right of survivorship - The right of survivorship is an attribute of several types of joint ownership of property, most notably joint tenancy and tenancy in common. When jointly owned property includes a right of survivorship, the surviving owner automatically absorbs a dying owner's share of the property. Thus if A and B jointly own a house with a right of survivorship, and B dies, A becomes the sole owner of the house, despite any contrary intent in B's will.

Secondary mortgage market - A secondary mortgage market is the market where mortgage loans and servicing rights are bought and sold between mortgage originators, mortgage aggregators (securitizers) and investors. The secondary mortgage market is extremely large and liquid.

Short-rate - The relatively higher insurance premium rate charged for coverage when one cancels a policy earlier than originally agreed upon. Rather than receiving a pro rata refund of the unearned premium,the property owner receives a smaller amount.

Standby commitment - A standby commitment is a formal agreement by a bank agreeing to lend money to a borrower up to a specified amount for a specific period. It is also known as firm commitment lending. The amount given under standby commitment is to be used only in specified contingency.

Subject to mortgage - circumstance in which a buyer takes title to mortgaged real property but is not personally liable for the payment of the amount due. The buyer must make payments in order to keep the property; however, with default, only the buyer's equity in that property is lost. Contrast assumption of mortgage.

Subordination - For an individual, the most frequent example of a subordination agreement is when an individual attempts to refinance the first mortgage on a property which has a second mortgage. The second mortgage has a lower priority than the first mortgage, but these priorities may be upset by refinancing the loan.

Supply and demand - The law of supply and demand is a basic economic principle that explains the relationship between supply and demand for a good or service and how the interaction affects the price of that good or service. The relationship of supply and demand affects the housing market and the price of a house

Tax lien - A tax lien is a lien imposed by law upon a property to secure the payment of taxes. A tax lien may be imposed for delinquent taxes owed on real property or personal property, or as a result of failure to pay income taxes or other taxes.

Tax shelter -Tax shelters can range from investments or investment accounts that provide favorable tax ... evasion, the illegal avoidance of taxes through misrepresentation or similar means. ... A tax shelter product designed to create large, seemingly real .

Tenancy by entirety - Tenants by entirety (TBE) is a method in some states by which married couples can hold the title to a property. In order for one spouse to modify his or her interest in the property in any way, the consent of both spouses is required by tenants by entirety.

Tenants-in-common - Tenancy in common is a type of shared ownership of property, where each owner owns a share of the property. Unlike in a joint tenancy, these shares can be of unequal size, and can be freely transfered to other owners both during life and via a will.

Title - a right or claim to the ownership of property or to a rank or throne.

Title insurance policy - Title insurance is an insurance policy that covers the loss of ownership interest in a property due to legal defects and is required if the property is under mortgage. The most common type of title insurance is a lender's title insurance, which is paid for by the borrower but protects only the lender.

Trust deed - a deed of conveyance creating and setting out the conditions of a trust

Usury - the illegal action or practice of lending money at unreasonably high rates of interest.

Vacancy and rent loss - Vacancy and Credit Loss in real estate investing is the amount of money or percentage of net operating income that is estimated to not be realized due to non-payment of rents and vacant units

Vacancy factor - The vacancy rate is the percentage of all available units in a rental property, such as a hotel or apartment complex, that are vacant or unoccupied at a particular time. It is the opposite of the occupancy rate, which is the percentage of units in a rental property that are occupied.

Warranty deed - a deed that guarantees a clear title to the buyer of real property.

Will - A will or testament is a legal document by which a person, the testator, expresses their wishes as to how their property is to be distributed at death, and names one or more persons, the executor, to manage the estate until its final distribution.

Without recourse - a formula used to disclaim responsibility for future nonpayment, especially of a negotiable financial instrument.

Wrap-around - "wrap", is a form of secondary financing for the purchase of real property. The seller extends to the buyer a junior mortgage which wraps around and exists in addition to any superior mortgages already secured by the property.

Please Leave a Great Review!

I have purchased all of the top real estate investing books on the market, and most have a handful of out dated web sites for their sources of properties.

There is not another real estate investing book on the market that gives you as many sources for wholesale real estate than this book.

My book gives you more and in most cases for less!

This book also gives you a web site that has over 4,000 sources of real estate financing in addition to the government's over 2,400 sources of Federal Assistance.

I have enjoyed doing all the research and sharing my real world real estate investing experience in what I hope is easy to understand terminology.

So I ask you to leave a honest and hopefully great review!

Thank you. Warm Regards,

Brian Mahoney

Get Our Video Training Program at:

**(Zero Cost Internet Marketing
complete 142 video series)
Amazing Training Videos!**

**YouTube Video Marketing
Email Marketing
Copy writing
Set up a Squeeze page
Getting Massive Web Traffic**

https://goo.gl/UFSIY6

Learn how to Get
Massive Money
for Real Estate Investing
@

http://www.BrianSMahoney.com

Join Our VIP Mailing List and Get FREE Money Making Training Videos! Then Start Making Money within 24 hours!
Plus if you join our Mailing list you can get Revised and New Edition versions of your book free!

And Notifications of other FREE Offers!

Just Hit/Type in the Link Below

https://mahoneyproducts.wixsite.com/win1

CPSIA information can be obtained
at www.ICGtesting.com
Printed in the USA
LVHW062335010623
748646LV00012B/341